Dragon
Hunter

The author
Keith Taylor
talks about the story

"*Dragon Hunter* is set in Iceland in the time of the Vikings, a place and time that has always interested me."

Dragon Hunter

It happened the year after Erik Thorvaldson—Erik the Red—left Iceland. That spring was warm. I was setting fish traps in the river near our farm, without a care in the world.

Then, a huge roar rolled over the land. The loudest thunderclap I'd ever heard paled in comparison. I lost my footing and went under the water. The racket was worse when I waded ashore.

The sky was turning dark.

My little sister, Signy, rushed out of the alders that grow beside the river. I hadn't known she was there. Her idea of fun in those days was to follow me around, spying on me. You would think that at ten years old she would have had more sense.

"Asmund!" she yelled. "What is it, what's happening?"

She was scared, all right. Normally she would have been squealing with laughter if she saw me slip

and take a ducking! Well, I couldn't answer her question. I'd never heard a volcano erupt before.

She answered her own question. "It's the Horn of Fate! Hemdall is blowing his trumpet. It's time for the world to end!"

"No, stupid," I said roughly. "It can't be. First there has to be a winter that lasts for years."

I wasn't sure, though. She could have been right. Gray ash had begun falling like snow by the time we reached home. Luckily my father had seen this before, and he told us that one of the fiery mountains must have erupted. I made fun of Signy all day for thinking that the end of the world had come.

The next day, the sky was still dim. The morning after that, a man, tall and carefree, came walking down the riverbank, past our barley fields. He carried a spear and an ax. Long, yellow hair fell down past his shoulders.

"It's Lidrek," my father said.

Signy was there, listening, and she spoke up, as usual. "Lidrek the outlaw?"

"Mind your own business, girl," Father said.

Signy was quiet, for once. She didn't want to be sent inside and miss seeing the famous outlaw. Her eyes were big and round.

9

Mine might have looked the same, if I'd let them. Instead, I narrowed them on purpose, and stood as tall as I could at fourteen years old. I wasn't going to seem afraid, even of Lidrek.

He whistled as he strode to our door.

"Good day, Thorgeir," he greeted my father. (They were on friendly terms.) "I've a thing to say that is best said at once. When the fire mountain erupted, it disturbed a dragon. It appears angry. Now, with luck it won't come this way, but I've warned you."

"A dragon," Father said. He pulled at his beard. "That's heavy news."

We believed him at once. Even Lidrek's enemies would admit he was truthful. Father, as the priest-chieftain of our district, called a meeting to which all of our neighbors came. By the time they arrived, the dragon had paid a visit to Thorsa River. It had slaughtered a flock of sheep and burned down a house.

"We must kill it!" someone said.

"Yes," Father agreed, "but I don't know who can do the deed."

"Except in stories, I don't know that anyone has ever killed one," Lidrek remarked, lounging against one of our hall pillars. "Still, a band of men might. I'll guide you to its lair, if Thorgeir goes."

Right away I called out that I would go and pointed out that I was big enough to be treated like a man. In the end, I got my way. Signy had a dream that night that made her wake up screaming, and she was very quiet when the dawn came. But we were so busy preparing to leave that none of us took much notice.

By Thor, we should have!

Twenty of us followed Lidrek north. Two days later, we reached a lava field with a shining glacier nearby. Across the frozen lava lay the volcano called Fire Giant's Mountain.

It wasn't big. The eruption had broken through its southwest side in a thick river of fire that was still shifting and cracking. We had to circle around to the east before we could go near.

"Watch your footing, all," Lidrek said. "It's easy to break your ankle among these rocks."

We had worse trouble than that in the next moment. The dragon swooped down on us suddenly, its wide mouth spewing fire. Its spread wings looked like huge, ribbed, green-gold leaves. Just the wind from them knocked strong men down. I dropped to one knee and held my shield in front of my face.

The dragon landed in a fury of claws and lashing tail. A spurred wing tip tossed me through the air.

When I got my breath back and looked, the bravest men I knew were running in all directions.

I didn't blame them. I agreed with Lidrek now. Except in stories, no one has ever destroyed a dragon. Rising, the dragon flew back to the volcanic mountain.

My breeches were singed and smoking. After beating the sparks out, I looked around the wide lava field for Father. Instead, I saw a small figure moving toward the foot of Fire Giant's Mountain. She had a determined step and wore a sky-blue, hooded cloak that I knew well.

It couldn't be Signy! She would have had to follow

us for two days without being seen, keeping up with a band of men. It wasn't possible. She was only ten years old.

Well, she was here, so she had done it. It was no use calling it impossible. I started running. She would not stop if I called out to her. Besides, the dragon might hear.

Late in the afternoon, I found her blue cloak outside a crevice in the peak, high on the mountain. Being bigger than Signy, I had a hard time forcing my way inside. The jagged rock scraped off yards of my skin.

The dragon's lair was a big lava cave that had suffered badly in the eruption. Masses of stone had fallen out of the roof, half of the rock floor had tilted away from the other half, and there was a deep crevice between them. Signy was nowhere to be seen, but the dragon crouched by the hole, looking down into it.

Then it turned its head and looked at me.

What would have happened next, I can't say. Most likely, it would have swallowed me in about three bites if Signy's head had not risen out of the hole at that moment. Her hair was tangled and gray with rock dust. She had a leathery egg as big as her body clutched in her arms and was rolling it up from the crack in the cave floor. The dragon caught it like a cat seizing a mouse and pulled it close against its scaly chest. Then it lay still once more.

"Signy!" I called out.

It surprised her to see me, but she wasted no time asking how I had arrived. "Brother! Help me bring up the last egg. That's what the dragon wants. Once we do that, she will be content and not burn any more farms or ships. But the eggs are so heavy."

It wasn't a time to argue. Signy seemed to know what she was talking about. I obeyed her, while the dragon watched me with angry, anxious, deadly eyes.

By Thor, it was not nearly as anxious as I!

One egg was still in the crevice. I squirmed down beside it and rolled it over. This one was terribly light, because the shell had broken, and its contents were gone. My guts turned to ice.

There was nothing to do but carry it up.

The dragon examined it with wise, dreadful eyes, then picked it up and saw the smashed underside. She let out a roar that shook the cave. Her tail coiled and lashed like a great whip. We're finished, I thought. But after another roar, she clutched the other eggs and lowered her head over them in protection. She let us depart when I took Signy's hand. We didn't delay, believe me.

By the time we reached the foot of the mountain, it was dark. Neither of us had said a word all of the way down, but now I asked, "Why did you follow us to the dragon's lair? And how did you know what to do?"

"I had a dream," she said. "It was so clear. I saw the dragon trying to get down into that rock cleft after her eggs, where they had fallen. But she was too big."

"That was the dream that made you wake up screaming in the night?"

"Yes. I saw that was why she was furious and

17

doing so much harm. I saw she would not stop until someone got the eggs back for her."

Her gray eyes were big and serious. She didn't seem like my teasing pest of a little sister anymore. Only prophets and seers have dreams like that. Signy had never shown signs of such a gift before, and no one else in our family had it.

"There's something else," she added.

"What?"

"The other eggs, the two I got before you came." Her voice trembled. "They were both cracked, Asmund. Not broken, but cracked. The dragon could notice it any moment now."

Signy and I looked at each other.

And we started running.

Dragon Fuel

The author
Paul Collins
talks about the story

"Dragons always get a raw deal. They're either holding maidens hostage and fighting gallant knights, or they're being slain. So the dragon in my story doesn't do any of that stuff. He's just hungry."

Dragon Fuel

It was just my luck to get caught by Lee Brookes on the way home from school. The sky was really dark—it was going to start pouring any second. If I walked past Brooksy, he'd get me for sure. If I took the long way home, I'd get drenched and muddy.

I kept walking along the sidewalk. Lee looked up when I got near him. As if he didn't know I was coming!

"What're you doing?" Brooksy kicked a rock my way. It flew between my feet and slammed into an iron fence.

I shrugged. "It's going to start pouring rain. Thought I might go home."

"You're such a loser, Tyson. You think a little rain's gonna hurt you?"

A bright flash cut through the gray clouds. A low rumble crawled across the sky. Rain was starting to dot the sidewalk.

"Check that out!" Brooksy shouted.

I turned just in time to see something fall from the sky. It was going really fast, like a rocket.

"Come on, Tyson! That could've been a meteorite or something. Cool!"

When Brooksy tells you to come on, you come on. He goes ballistic otherwise. But Mom would lose it if I came home drenched. Too many decisions to make in one day.

We were both soaked by the time we reached the park. Lightning sliced the sky, and the thunder was the loudest I'd ever heard.

I found the dragon first. I could see a pile of earth right in the middle of the field. It looked like someone had been digging a grave. Or maybe a bomb had hit the park.

I looked into the hole. "Hey Brooksy, look what I found!"

I bent over to get a closer look at the dragon.

Brooksy rushed over. Rain plastered his hair to his scalp. He looked like something out of a horror movie. He's got crazy eyes. You know the type, a real terrorist.

Brooksy's eyes widened. "Cool!" He slid into the hole.

"It's mine," I said feebly.

Brooksy didn't bother to look up. "I touched it first. Yeouchh!!!"

I jumped backward. I can't tell you how loud he screamed.

Brooksy kicked at the dragon and screamed again. Then he climbed back out. "It bit me!"

I peered down at the dragon. A streak of lightning lit the hole. The dragon looked like it was made from cast iron.

Brooksy saw my look of disbelief. He clenched his fists.

"I didn't say anything!" I said. "If you say it bit you, that's good enough for me."

Brooksy sucked on his fingers. "You stand guard, Tyson. The dragon's mine. I'll come back with a wheelbarrow."

So there I was out in the middle of the park, guarding a cast-iron dragon for Lee Brookes. He limped home. I bet I was there for a good hour. By then, I was shivering and wet to the skin. If I lost Brooksy's dragon, I'd be dead meat. If I stayed here all night, I'd be some kind of moron.

So I scrambled into the hole. I was ready to run if the dragon opened its mouth. But like I said, it was made from cast iron. Brooksy was seriously ill if he really thought it had bitten him.

It was icy cold and heavy, and for the first time in the history of the planet, someone, namely me, wished Brooksy was there with his wheelbarrow.

Mom met me at the front door. "*What* were you doing out there in this weather, Tyson? And *look* at you!"

"I got a present for you and Dad," I lied. "It's heavier than I thought." I panted a bit. "It took me a long time to walk home with it." I dropped it like a rock next to the gas fireplace.

"You got that for us?" Mom said. She looked astonished. "It must have cost a bundle. I've never seen anything like it."

"It's unique," I admitted.

My kid sister, Jasmine, poked her tongue out. "You're such a kiss-up, Tyson."

It upsets Jasmine majorly when I score points with Mom. I smirked at her and left them studying the dragon. I needed dry clothing. By the time I got back, Mom had given the dragon a good cleaning.

Dad was impressed with their present. He kept looking over at it, almost as though he expected it to get up and breathe some fire.

That night, I kept worrying that Brooksy was going to call and claim I'd stolen his dragon. When I heard a noise downstairs, I knew it had to be Brooksy.

I freaked at the thought of going downstairs and facing him. No one, but no one, takes Lee Brookes on. There was a scraping noise and a crunching noise. I expected to hear Mom or Dad barreling down the stairs. All I could hear was Dad's snoring.

Brooksy's dragging the dragon across the carpet, I thought. When in doubt, stay in bed.

I did.

Mom knocked on my door early the next morning. "Tyson, did you wreck your sister's doll?"

I forced my eyes open. Mom was holding what looked like a mop. "What doll?" I asked stupidly.

Mom waved the mop. "This is what's left of her Daring Darlene doll."

"Maybe the cat did it."

"Tyson?"

"Daring Dan, maybe?"

Mom went back downstairs to console Jasmine.

Why would Brooksy have wrecked Jasmine's doll? Maybe he'd stepped on it in the dark? I got dressed quickly and checked out the dragon.

It was still there on the hearth. Now *that* was a mystery.

I went to school expecting major hassles from Brooksy. But nothing! The ape had forgotten all about the dragon. Sometimes you can worry yourself sick for no reason.

I slept better that night, until about 5 a.m., that is. Then I heard bumping, crunching, and scratching sounds coming from downstairs.

I crept downstairs. I'm not normally a hero, and I seriously thought of pounding on Mom and Dad's bedroom door. But for some reason, I didn't.

That's when I saw the dragon munching on Dad's *Star Wars* videotape. Dad would freak if he knew what was happening to his favorite movie.

Without thinking, I rushed into the room. The dragon heard me and slowly waddled across the living room floor. It heaved itself onto the hearth.

I picked up Dad's mangled video.

"Who's down there?"

Yikes! Dad! I dropped *Star Wars* like a hot potato and hid behind the TV.

There was silence for a moment. Then I heard Dad talking to Mom with their door closed. My legs were shaking. If Dad had found me holding his wrecked tape, I would be in big trouble.

I slid out from behind the TV and crept over to where the dragon sat. Right now you're thinking I must be crazy, right? Cast-iron dragons don't move. They don't eat plastic. Not to mention that there's no such thing as a dragon, right? Wrong, on all counts.

I touched the dragon. Instead of being icy cold, it had a slight warmth to it.

I pushed at it, jiggled it, blew on it, but nothing happened. It just sat there, like a lump of cast iron.

"Okay, if that's the way you want it," I whispered, "that's fine." I got up and crept upstairs to bed. I thought of tying up the dragon with an old sheet. But if its teeth were real, nothing would hold it.

The next morning I heard a mighty roar from Dad.

"Tyson! Come down here this instant!"

I got up quickly. So the video-eating incident hadn't been a nightmare. I was in for it now.

"Tyson!"

"Coming!" I rushed downstairs in my pajamas.

"How many times have I told you to leave my videos alone, Tyson?"

"Dad—I didn't touch it!"

"You're such a liar," Jasmine said.

"Excuse me? Butthead." Jasmine's such a nerd.

"Tyson? Answer me."

30

"You don't understand!"

"Darn right I don't," Dad snapped. "And look at the mess down here. What on earth were you doing last night?"

I widened my eyes. There were pieces of chewed plastic littering the living room floor. The dragon had wrecked some of my CD-ROM cases.

"Someone must've broken in last night," I said.

"Sure," Jasmine said.

"Shut up, Jasmine," Dad said. "Tyson, get the vacuum cleaner and clean up this mess. I'll be reducing your allowance for the next month over this."

Jasmine was happy. She waved at me and fled the room. I vacuumed in silence, glaring at the dragon.

The moment the bell rang for lunch, I went to the library. Then I stayed behind after school and checked out the Internet. There were thousands of sites about dragons.

The most fascinating thing I noticed was that dragons fed on coal. Of course, there weren't any coal mines around home. But why would the dragon eat plastic? I surfed the Net and found what I was looking for. Duh. And double-duh! Plastic is made from coal and oil!

I smacked my head. The dragon was hungry. It couldn't get warm unless it ate. But at the rate it was going, it'd eat us out of house and home. I only got so much allowance in a year.

If it stayed cold, it wouldn't be able to move. I could lock it in the fridge at night, but I wouldn't be so cruel. The dragon was a living creature. But the warmer it got, the more it would move around the house, and soon I wouldn't be getting any allowance.

This problem needed some serious thought.

Brooksy was lurking at his favorite spot. I'd have to walk the long way home to get past him.

By the time I got home, I knew exactly what to do.

Mom and Dad weren't due home for two hours. I wrapped the dragon in a blanket and balanced it on my bike seat. It took half an hour to reach the town dump.

The seagulls were curious. They wheeled about overhead, squawking. I waited until no one was looking and tipped the dragon into a pile of trash.

I watched it tumble head over tail. It came to rest by some plastic sheeting. I must have blinked, because the next second it was burrowing into the plastic.

Well, easy come, easy go.

I got an earful from Mom and Dad that night. They had decided it was my fault that the door had been left open and someone had come in and stolen that antique dragon. I tried putting the blame on Jasmine—after all, she left home after me this morning. But for some reason, I always get the blame. I'm the oldest, after all.

But let me tell you something. I visit the dump once a

week. It's amazing how many coins and pieces of jewelry I find, right where I let the dragon go. You know, treasure—from a dragon's hoard.

It's payment, I think, for saving a dragon's life.

Two
Dragons

The author
Peter Friend
talks about the story

"What if dragons are real? What if
they've been hiding for hundreds of
years, counting their treasure, patiently
waiting for the opportunity to take us
over? I thought they might turn out to
be very nice."

Two Dragons

"Take your clothes off, please, sir," a guard told Jax.

He'd never been called "sir" before—usually it was "kid" or "boy" or worse. Not many people said "please" either. Then again, most folks didn't make him strip.

The guards took his little, silver dragon statue and most of his clothes, but let him keep his underpants. Then they waved scanners and tech-sniffers all over him and his stuff. And then they x-rayed him a couple of times, just in case.

There was nothing for them to find, except the surgical pin in his shinbone from when he'd broken his leg years ago.

So far, everything was going according to plan.

The guards gave Jax back his silver dragon, and

when he looked up, there was the real dragon. It was at least ten feet tall, with skin like polished leather and breath like burned paper. The dragon picked up the statue, stared, blinked, and licked it. Then the dragon bent down and looked at Jax.

"Fascinating. Do you know what this is, young Jax?" The dragon had a high, raspy voice, sounding almost human.

"Not exactly, Lord Reptile," said Jax. "But everyone knows you like silver, and everyone knows you like dragons. So when I found that statue, I thought of you."

"How very kind," said the dragon, sounding a little sarcastic.

"It's a genuine antique, worth tons," said Jax, trying to sound confident.

"This is no antique, little boy. Look, you can see the laser lines on its base."

Jax felt the sweat in his armpits turning cold.

"Probably made right here in town," continued the dragon, "using tools and silver stolen from my mines. You stole it, and now you're trying to sell it to me."

"I didn't steal it," mumbled Jax, closing his eyes and waiting to die.

The dragon rattled its wings.

"I could just throw you over the town walls. Which would kill you first, do you think, the pollution or the wild dogs? Or, I could have you tied to the girders above the market square, then breathe flame over you. That would remind everyone who runs this town."

"But instead, I'll let you live. The statue is charming, quite charming. I'll even pay you for it. And in return, you'll tell me who made it."

"My mother made the statue, Lord Reptile. She's dead."

"Ah. My deepest sympathy on your sad loss—and my sad loss. I'll have to check that you're not lying. But if she's dead, I suppose I can't blame you for that. So, what do you want for the statue? Five hundred credits?"

"Most generous, Lord Reptile," said Jax. It was double what he'd expected. "But I'd hoped that . . . um . . ."

"You'd rather look at my treasure room."

Jax nodded.

The dragon sighed. "Everyone says that. Very well, you can go through the door on your left. Don't be greedy."

The door creaked open, then closed behind him. Jax was alone in the dragon's treasure room. There was probably more wealth here than in the rest of the town put together. There were gold and silver coins. A glass bowl full of rings—the dragon claimed all jewelry worn by anyone who died in town. Stacks of knives and forks, necklaces, picture frames, earrings, nose rings, buttons—even a soccer trophy, dated nearly a hundred years ago.

And no one to watch him? It was obviously a trap, and he wouldn't fall for it. He had to get out of here alive; otherwise, this was all a waste of time.

Everything was polished and shining. The townspeople said the dragon sat here every night, polishing everything itself. That was its only idea of fun, they said.

Jax started sorting through the bowl of rings. He found the first one easily—it had a tiny ruby, a diamond, then another ruby. Dad, on the other hand, had never liked gemstones. Jax had to check dozens of plain gold rings before he found the one with the faint spiral pattern he remembered.

Then he reached up, as if interested in a silver-plated videophone on a nearby shelf, and pretended to fall onto a pile of forks. As he'd planned, he cut his shin. It really did hurt. He didn't have to fake shouting for the hidden cameras. Carefully, he pressed down on his leg in three places and felt more pain as the surgical pin in his shin did its special work.

"Have a little accident?" asked the dragon, when he returned a few minutes later.

"Sorry, I'm clumsy," said Jax, wiping the blood from his leg. "I'll clean it up if—"

"Don't bother," interrupted the dragon. "Why pick just those two rings? They're pretty enough, but hardly valuable."

"My parents' wedding rings."

"How touching. I guess I'm just a sweet old reptile today. Guards, x-ray him again to make sure he didn't swallow anything, then give him two hundred credits before he goes. And Jax, if you come across any other dragonish family heirlooms, come back and see me, won't you?"

"I'll return. I promise, Lord Reptile."

Back in the treasure room, the drops of Jax's blood quivered. Out crawled hundreds of tiny machines smaller than fleas. Microbots were nothing unusual—millions of them worked in the dragon's mines—but these were different.

They jumped and hurried through the shadows. Although they were too small for the security cameras to see, they weren't completely safe. Several were crippled by spiders that mistook them for real insects. Ten were crushed under the boots of a passing guard. One was squashed by a falling fork.

But microbots were designed to work in large numbers. By nightfall, they were delicately drilling into computer cables throughout the room.

In an empty building two blocks from the dragon's palace, two people watched a video screen. Jax's microbots were sending it the same images as those on the dragon's security cameras. The picture flickered and buzzed, but was clear enough to show what was happening.

At midnight, the dragon entered the treasure room. The rumors were true—it spent the next hour polishing its treasure and looking at the blood-spattered forks.

At last, it left.

"You don't have to do this, Jax," said the old woman.

"Yes, I do, Gran," said Jax. He kissed her cheek and left.

He checked his equipment harness once more and threw a hook over the palace wall. No alarms sounded, no spotlights glared, no lasers shone red dots onto his chest. The microbots had done their work, jamming sensors and video signals. The dragon's computers would see nothing but the empty night.

Jax climbed the rope and dropped down inside the wall, looking out for guards. Video cameras continued to ignore him, and doors opened for him as he approached. Five minutes later, after avoiding two guards—humans this time—he was in the treasure room again.

He checked the power levels of his equipment harness, switched on a headlight, and picked up a large, silver bowl.

"Lights," said a high, raspy voice behind him, and the room lit up. "It's so much easier to find things with the lights on, don't you think, Jax?"

"Yes, Lord Reptile," Jax said, not bothering to turn around.

"My boy, I've ruled this town for two hundred years, ever since the Gene Wars put you ridiculous humans back in your proper place. Do you really think you're the first to try stealing my treasure or the first to try using microbots to jam my security systems? I designed those microbots myself. And my computer system has kept track of them ever since they jumped out of your leg. The fake surgical pin was an original touch, I admit. And I adored the little dragon statue. Did your mother really make it?"

"Yes, Lord Reptile. Three weeks before you killed her and Dad."

"Killed them? Me?"

"They were part of the miners' strike last year. You blew up the mine shaft and buried twenty people alive, remember?"

"Oh, yes, that was a shame. We lost two days' production. And I hate wasting valuable workers, which I'm sure your dear parents were. Now put down that bowl, Jax, and be careful. It really is an antique. Then raise your hands and turn around. You're a clever boy, and I may let you live."

"Thank you, Lord Reptile." Jax turned and raised his arms, triggering the equipment on the front of his harness. A dozen tiny missiles leaped at the dragon. The mining explosives in their warheads ripped deep holes in its scaly chest.

The missile recoil knocked Jax back into the wall. He couldn't move his left arm, and his ribs were in agony. He grinned at the guards and pointed to the dragon's body oozing black blood onto the floor.

"Lord Reptile is dead. You can kill me, but ask yourselves this: shouldn't we humans be running this town for ourselves now?"

And then he fainted.

About the Illustrators

The Story Illustrator
Marilyn Pride

Marilyn Pride has illustrated several books on dinosaurs. Recently she has been working on realistic creatures for natural history books, so she was pleased to have the chance to draw some dragons. "I enjoyed trying out various black and white techniques, and especially designing the creature in *Two Dragons*. I saw it more as an 'evolved dinosaur' than a traditional dragon, as the story has a strong science fiction slant."

The Cover Illustrator
Marc McBride

Marc McBride has illustrated covers for several magazines and children's books. Marc currently creates the realistic images for his covers using acrylic ink with an airbrush. To solve his messy studio problem, he plans to use computer graphics instead.